Is
This
It?

SERENA PATEL

Cover Art By: Anjalina D. Patel
anjal02.patel@gmail.com

ISBN: 0692848231
ISBN-13: 978-0692848234

IS THIS IT?

SERENA PATEL

Dedicated to Suvrat Rao —

I am not sure if you will ever see this, but thank you. Six years ago, you gave me the greatest gift. You made my dreams a reality and gave me a taste of what could be. I will never forget that.

ACKNOWLEDGMENTS

Thank you to all those who have inspired, supported, and helped me throughout the process – *especially N.D.T., K.M.U., N.K.S., A.D.P., K.R.S., K.S.S., S.R.S.. P.P.K, R.S.M., S.P., and Kona*. Thank you for giving me time you did not have. Without you, this would not be what it is.

SERENA PATEL

IS THIS IT?

My Original Cover Letter

Dear Whom It May Concern:

What does a consultant by trade say when she submits a book of poetry? I "advise" you to give me a shot; it will be a worthwhile "investment." You also get a terrible joke.

When I was younger, and writers or artists caught my attention – like Thoreau or Nietzsche – I would search for hundreds of their most famous quotes. I thought that sometimes a few words could say more about a person or an idea than an entire novel. That sometimes a few words could hold more weight when they weren't covered in fluff or draped in drama. And sometimes, those bare words extended far beyond their intended meaning.

Before you is a collection of pieces that have stemmed from thoughts inspired by quotes, lyrics, and art. Each piece is strung together by an overarching story of a poet who writes to recover, but is held back by the same thing that helps her as she must relive the pain through her writing.

The answer is yes – yes, there are more qualified writers out there. There are people who have spent years and have earned degrees studying poetry and the art of writing. I could tell you that I am different, but isn't everyone? What it comes down to is that this is *my* perspective. No matter how many degrees someone holds in English or

Philosophy from some prestigious university, these are *my* experiences and no one else can perfectly or authentically replicate that.

People want to read things they can find pieces of themselves in. People want to be represented by someone like them. I am that minority. I am that female. I am that millennial. I am that artist. I am that everyday person with a day job and a night passion.

Thank you,
Serena Patel

SERENA PATEL

"Nothing ever ends poetically.
It ends and we turn it into poetry.
All that blood was never once beautiful.
It was just red."

— Kait Rokowski

SERENA PATEL

"When a poet digs himself into a hole,
He doesn't climb out.
He digs deeper, enjoys the scenery,
And comes out of the other side enlightened."

— Criss Jami

IS THIS IT?

"This morning
With her
Having coffee."
— Johnny Cash *when asked his definition of Paradise.*

You
By my side.

Reading in bed
Kisses on my forehead.

We were at ease when
We only had each other to please.

— My Paradise was you.

He used to say
I am infatuated
With beautiful girls —
Especially you.

Your big brown eyes
Your button nose
The way your curls bounce
When the wind blows.

How your delicate little hand
Always finds mine
As if that's where
It was meant to be.

How when you smile big
Or laugh out loud
Your eyes nearly close.

When I pick you up
To hug you
I feel like
I could crush your bones.

I am afraid
My infatuation
Is becoming
Something more.

— He used to call me his pretty girl.

The words slipped out…
                    … so effortlessly.

Without thought
Without force.

Lingering,
          Laying,
                    Waiting
To be heard.

— When I first said I loved you.

When I caught her smile
I cannot explain what I felt.

A love like that is too deep
Too beautiful
To ever dull or ruin
By trying to capture in words.

— Kona

My thoughts kept drifting to
Tangled legs in unkempt beds
The air was so light
You could see the dust float through.

We lay on our sides
Facing each other
As I held your hand
With both of mine
Tracing the creases
Of your skin.

My head was happy
My chest was full.

I could live in that moment
Forever satisfied with
Whatever life was
Without understanding its purpose
Or asking why
Living eternally in my ignorant bliss.

— I could waste whole days like this.

In the dark
Streetlight peering through
He smelled like whiskey
He smelled like lies too.

> *Smoking cigarettes*
> *In silence*
> *Long drags*
> *Slow blinks*
> *Soft sounds*
> *Around the room.*

Nights like those
Said more than
We ever could.

—— Will you remember how we sat here like this?

Lie by lie
The truth
Unraveled.

Piece by piece
Our world
Fell apart.

— And that was just the start.

"Hey
Must be a devil between us
Or whores in my head."
      — Pixies, *Hey*

Whores
Whores in your bed.

But hey
Haven't there always been?

You always win
With that smile
As you try to crawl
Under my skin.

I try to go
But it works
I'm stuck
Standing here
Watching you
Be with her.

      — You don't do this to someone you say you love.

In the Beat of "Is This It" by The Strokes

Crying, screaming, shouting
We don't know what went wrong
But we are fighting
How could this be it?

Pushing, pulling, trying
But we are not in sync
So we start drowning
Desperate to hold on.

How did we end up like this?
You were only supposed to stay
A couple of days
But seasons passed.

Running, falling, crawling
Reaching for the door
I just can't do this anymore
It wasn't supposed to be like this.

Do you remember that old rhyme?
The one that goes…

"Humpty Dumpty sat on a wall.
Humpty Dumpty had a great fall.
All the King's horses and all the King's men
Couldn't put Humpty together again."

Except…

Humpty didn't sit on a wall
Loving you was my greatest fall
What was I thinking when I gave you my all
When you wouldn't even answer my calls?

All attempts by all other men
All the words written by my pen
All the time spent waiting for 'when'
Couldn't put my heart together again.

— Humpty Dumpty wasn't an egg.

I'm sorry, but there is no
'If it was meant to be, it will happen eventually.'
That's not how life works.
There is no invisible force pushing things or people together.
Haven't you lived long enough to realize
That if you want something
You have to work for it?

There is no right time or right place.
There is no 'maybe someday in the future.'
There are only excuses.
I can't just wait for things fall into place.

If you aren't willing to make it work right now
Why would I want you to have me when it's easy?
I want someone who wants me even when it's hard
Because they think I'm worth it.

The longer you keep coming up with reasons of why not to
The farther we grow apart,
The more we change,
And it only becomes more certain
That we will never be the same.

So I'm sorry that our love is inconvenient for you at this time,
But when you're finally ready or realize what you've lost
I'll be long gone.

    — As Tupac said,
        "That's just the way it is.
        Things will never be the same."

I can't feel a thing
And I'm terrified.

I should be screaming,
       crying,
      fighting

            with you,

But I'm not.

I should feel hurt
      broken,
      defeated,
But I don't.

I don't feel a single thing
As I sit with my back
Against the cold wall
Staring out in front of me
          at
          absolutely
          nothing
          at all.

—— This is what it means to feel dead inside.

You don't abandon
Something that is broken
And hope it'll just fix itself.

> *Time*
> *Alone*
> *Does*
> *Nothing.*

— You don't abandon people either.

There was once a girl
Who had the whole world
Endless possibilities
As she was told.

Then she grew up
Life became a little rough
The world wasn't what
She imagined it to be.

Those endless possibilities?
Promises —
Far from reach.

— It always starts with
Once upon a time.

"Fool me once,
Shame on you.
Fool me twice,
Shame on me."

Fool me three times?
Four?
Five?
Six?
Who's to blame?
Society?
For making me
So naive?

For letting little kids believe
Lying and cheating are routine?
For encouraging acting carelessly
Instead of valuing integrity?

If you fool me
Ever again
I will ruin you
Right then.

— Fool me, I dare you.

Sadness never sleeps
At any time it might start to creep.

It is the monster in my bed.
It is the monster inside my head.

— Tonight I lay awake.

Maybe I can't sleep
Because my mind
Is trying to keep
You away from me

— In my dreams.

It is 2 a.m. and I am
            desperate for words
            desperate to be heard.

I want these words
            to bleed through the page.

When you touch them
            I want them to burn.

I want your blood to run
            as cold as my heart.

There are no pretty words
            when feelings have been hurt.

— I want you to feel this.

When all sanity is lost
You'll know where to find me...

— In my darkest thoughts.

When you love something
You don't risk letting it
Get too far away.

— You don't love me.

I don't want you on my mind
I don't want thoughts of you
Consuming my time.

I started to drink
So I wouldn't have to think
About who you might
Be flirting with tonight.

— I don't want to know.

If I was told six years ago how much I would change
If I was told everything that would happen to me
And what I would go through
If I was told who I was to become
I would not have believed it…

…not a single word.

It must be true
That we become who we least expect to.

— We become a danger to ourselves.

22,
But worn with age,
              experience,
              life.

Beaten black and blue
Heart untrusting
Blood cold
Mind restless.

— Ambition Fading

There is this strange feeling in my throat
And the back of my mind.

There are words that I'm searching for
That I can't seem to find.

There is an emptiness that surrounds me,
But I don't know why.

The tip of my pen is pressed against the page,
But my words are dry.

There is a writer in my chair,
But her head's up in the sky.

There is a story I am waiting to tell,
But I don't know what it is that I want to say.

Sometimes it's not until the middle
That you find where you should begin.

— Somewhere along the way
I'll find where I should be.

Maybe you were given to me
So I could write.

Maybe that's why
Our paths crossed.

Maybe you were meant to be
Taken away.

I always knew
I needed to share my story.

— I just didn't know that
My story would be you.

The sun will rise again,

But until it does
I'll have something
To write about.

— I am painting with blood from my wounds.

I stare at a blank sheet
                    with passion
                    with rage.

With words filling my head
Ready to fill the page.

My greatest fear
Is that I won't do it justice
With the words I choose.

So I carefully pick —

                    Crafting,
                    Sculpting

My memories
With the tip of my pen
Detailing every loop.

I write the way
An artist paints…

— Delicately.

Do you know what it's like to
Live through a love that has killed parts of you?

It is every feeling you have ever felt
Every feeling you could ever imagine.

— And somehow it's more.

I like to play pretend
            pretend that everything is fine
            pretend that I'm okay you're not mine.

— Do you want to play pretend?
    Do you want to make believe?

I write
So I don't have to fight
With these feelings anymore.

When I write
Things seem like
They may eventually
Be alright.

— This is why.

I am just patiently waiting
For the day I am fully okay
With how everything ended up.

— But isn't everyone?

I will keep you in my dreams
Until I can set you free...

— Trapped

Every step I take
You begin to fade away
So I stop moving.

I close my eyes
Reach out in front of me
Tracing the air –
I feel you underneath.

I run my fingers
Down your nose
Across your cheeks
Brushing your lips.

We are so far
But I feel you there
That's all I need.

— So I am left standing still.

It was deeper than the ocean
More mysterious too
Stung worse than salt
In open wounds
No matter how hard I tried
It couldn't be entirely understood.

It was so beautiful
At a distance or
Embraced by the waves
Pulling me in
Currents swallowing me whole
Cold slapping against my body
Yet I never wanted to leave.

— But I couldn't stay.

"If a writer falls in love with you,
You can never die."
— Mik Everett

It's true.
I kept our love alive
With the words on these pages.

But no matter how hard
I try or what I write
It doesn't change the truth.

On these pages you were sweeter
Our conversations were deeper
Our passion was fuller
Our lust never went to sleep.

I may exaggerate our story
For the sake of writing
                    I must,
But the one thing that was real
And will always be real
                    is us.

— I made you immortal.

*You were not given people
So you could keep them.*

*The faster you learn this
The less disappointed you'll be.*

— People were meant to leave.

When I learned
How to control my feelings
By controlling my thoughts
I learned how to be content
With silence.

> *To sit*
> *To stare*
> *To think*
> *Nothing*
> *At all.*

— I grew numb.

I learned from the last time
To walk
Not to run.

So I walked
        Carefully,
               Cautiously,
                       Guarded.

I didn't dress myself
With my heart
Worn on my sleeve.

Instead I kept the pieces
Safe in golden cages
Hidden in tiny reminders
With the locks lost

    — Somewhere deep inside.

He fills the empty space
So I stay.

I'd be lying if I said
I didn't need someone.

— I know I'll only end up hurting him too.

I love you
He said.

No you don't
You just think you do.

You're getting love
And lust confused.

You can't love me
When I don't love me.

> — That's not how it works
> I need to love myself first.

There is something
Very beautiful
In the consistency of knowing
That after every night
The sun will rise again.

There is something
So very beautiful
In knowing that no matter
What may leave
That is the one thing
That will always
Come back.

— Even when you won't.

People spend lifetimes
Trying to figure out the why's
They spend hours getting high
Contemplating time.

Children dream
Of breaking the circle of routine
Adults write stories
Of the masses breaking free.

We search for light – for purpose
We search for ourselves
We try to create sense of this chaotic mess
We think we are doing good
By trying to disrupt society.

You come home
Your lights won't turn on
Your water won't run
You wake up and realize
Getting high all the time and
Coming up with revelations
Doesn't pay the bills.

—— This is why I have a day job.

Everyday
I have given myself the ability
To relive all the best
And worst feelings
That have ever made me.

Some days it makes me feel alive
Other days it is in my memories
I hide

> *From reality*
> *From the truth*
> *From all things I cannot change.*

— It is both a blessing and a curse.

It's our fall
That created this all —
        This perfectly chaotic mess.

Without it
Would you have even realized
        Its beauty?
Would you have ever looked back
        And seen its grace?

What we had
What we were
Was beautiful.

        — Even if we didn't make it out alive.

Sometimes I imagine
Seeing you again,
But with the wisdom
I've grown to have.

You would walk through the door
As I sat at the bar
And happened to be looking
In that direction.

You would catch my eye
Hold my gaze
As you made your way
Through the crowded room.

I would hold my look
A second too long
Just in case
Your eyes were to meet mine too.

When they finally did
You would stare
I would wonder what you were thinking
When seeing me after so long.

— I wonder how much love is lost
Because of those who were too afraid
To do more than just look.

There were no worries in mind
                              when
                      I was yours
                          and

— You were mine.

They say
Love is fleeting.

No.

Passion is fleeting.

— Love lasts too damn long.

After I put my pen down
I never want to think of you again.

— I just want it to end.

I woke up one day
It finally sat with me
You didn't miss me
The fight was through
I couldn't do anything
To hold onto you.

I had to remind myself
From here and every day on
Time didn't stop for me
If I didn't let things go
I'd become stuck.

— I needed to start living again.

I apologize –
I apologize for the burden I put on you.

— I'm sorry I was too heavy to carry.

You can't force something
That isn't there.

You can't sculpt people
To be who you want them to be.

It is either enough as is
Or not.

— This time it was not.

I waited
At the
Edge
Of the
World.

I waited
For
Someone
To
Decipher
My words.

— I'm still waiting.

I picked up a handful of sand
And watched as it fell through
The emptiness between my fingers.

Forgive yourself
For the things that slipped through the cracks
While you watched.

— One person can't hold everything together.

It's been a long time
But every now and then
Something will happen
That will remind me of you
It'll make me wonder
If you ever think about me too.

— I like to believe you do.

The Reading

First Question:
What inspired you?
It seems to be about someone,
But who?

I smiled
And looked away
Down at the book in my hand.

It was about so many people
Stories and memories melted together.

Second Question:
When I read it
I really connected to it.
I was going through a breakup
And those were my thoughts and feelings.
Did it help you with the same thing?

In my mind I wanted to say no –
No
Because here I am right now
Sitting in front of you
Still talking about it.

I wanted to say that writing
Any of it was a mistake
Because now there was no escape.

But instead I said
Yes.

Third Question:
Are you happy now?

I raised my head
To see who asked
My eyes met his
While moments passed.

My head dropped low,
So he stood up to go.

The Interview

How does it feel to know that she's writing about you?
Or rather - for you?
You must be flattered.

Honestly,
I believe art is comprised of tragedies.
It is what makes it soulful —
When you feel the highs and lows.
It wouldn't be a tragedy
If it wasn't first beautiful.

If you're asking me if
I'd rather she write for me,
Or not give it a thought?
I'd rather she forgot.

I can't imagine what it's like
For her to hold onto this
To hold onto us
After so long
To hold onto things that break her heart
To have to read it
And reread it
To keep these memories alive
So she has feelings to paint with.

I think Chuck Palahniuk said it best,
"People fall so in love with their pain,
They can't leave it behind.
The same as the stories they tell.
We trap ourselves."

So no,
It isn't flattering
Like you thought.

Even after all these months
When I picked up the phone
To hear your voice
My walls crumbled
My tears crashed.

— Everything I built
Broke.

We met up for coffee
For the first time in years.

My stomach turned
When you walked in
Peered around the room
Spotted me and smiled.

It was that smile
That used to break my heart
A thousand times a day.

You sat across from me
I started to feel uneasy
I immediately knew why

When I looked into your eyes
What looked back was
Not someone I knew.

It was distant…
                    … unfamiliar…
It was then I realized
We had become strangers.

— It was just coffee.

People are not who you
Remember them to be.

The person you miss
No longer exists.

They only live
In your memory.

— That is where they are meant to stay.

You told me of
How happy you were –
Both were – together.

I heard your words
But my mind couldn't help
But to wonder why
If you were so happy
You were still calling me.

— Does she know?

Finally, I heard it
The words I was waiting for.

I've missed you.

But it didn't sit with me
The way I thought it would.

I didn't feel lightheaded
My life didn't fall into place.

I did feel something new though
I felt happy
                    I felt free.

Because for the first time…

— I only needed me.

Sometimes it takes getting what you want
To realize you no longer want it.

— Sometimes it's too late.

She doesn't know the truth
But we'll keep it as our last secret.

I like that.

— I get to keep a little part of you.

I was sucked into the past
I felt so much I almost forgot
That this was no longer me.

So I said what I thought I'd never mean
And asked for you to stay away.

— It is best for both of us.

It comes down to the truth —
That "our" world
      revolves
           only around you.

— I respect myself enough to walk away.

How did it all end?

So many people are sadly mistaken
When they see me
And ask this question.

They are always hoping
For something more.

The truth is
There is not always a
Meaningful exchange of words
Sometimes it ends with
Nothing more to be said.

— Not all endings are significant.

I finished the chapter
I closed the book
Somehow it feels like
A good place to end.

I don't know if I want to
Find out what happens after
So instead I lay content
With this beautiful new end.

— Sometimes you need to close the book.

There is no easy way to end things
There just isn't.

But there comes a time
When you realize that life moves on.

— So do people.

I said
I will love you
Until the sun
Is blue.

But instead
I loved you
Until my heart
No longer could.

— I tried.

Why is the grass green?
How did the universe become to be?
What happened in between?
Why were you not meant for me?

There is always an explanation
Behind every unknown
Even if we never find out
In this lifetime
And even if we never come
To fully understand.

— There is a reason behind everything.

You have taught me
How to forgive.

So…

I forgive you.

I forgive your actions —
Your mistakes.

I forgive what happened.

I forgive it all.

I forgive the past.

I forgive that
We weren't meant
To last.

But most importantly,
I forgive myself
For taking so long
To end things.

— For holding on when I should have let go.

I would like to say
Thank you.

Thank you
For pushing me away.

By breaking me down,
I've learned to be softer,
To love myself,
Treat myself right,
For once
Put myself first.

I've learned to recognize
The beauty in all things —
Including myself.

I am not bitter with you,
Or love,
Or the world.

Surprisingly
I have not lost hope.

— I just hope for different things now.

I don't know if I believe in destiny —
That certain things are meant to be
That space and time are only dust
And things end up as they must.

See. I used to believe in you and me
Until I realized that happiness came
Wherever I let happiness be.

— There is no inevitable ending.

"Thank you for the tragedy.
I need it for my art."
— Kurt Cobain

Thank you for your lies
I need it for my start.

Thank you for the pain
It made me fall apart.

Thank you for not trying
I couldn't feel my heart.

Thank you for our tragedy
For this wisdom I impart.

— This is tattooed in my mind.

After everything,
I am not scared of love
I do not hide.

For love has made me feel
The most beautiful
and tragic feelings
humanly possible.

Love has given me something to write about
While leaving me at a loss for words.

— During all that time
I felt so alive.

IS THIS IT?

I am lucky to have felt
               all that I felt.

— For some never experience that in a lifetime.

95

So many assume
I wrote this for someone.

I didn't write this for you
I wrote this for many,
But above all
I wrote this for me.

I wrote this because
I needed to remind myself
That after months and months
Of begging for you
To come back and fix me
All along
I was capable of fixing myself.

I never needed you
Or some miracle
To save me.

I smashed together the pieces of my soul
Until I felt whole.

— I wrote this for me.

Charles Bukowski said,
"Find what you love
And let it kill you."

No.

Find what you love,
But don't let it kill you.

What you love
Shouldn't have to destroy
Who you are.

No matter what you may love
Always love yourself more.

— Charles Bukowski was a great poet,
But he was wrong about a lot of things.

From all this
I've learned
The true beauty
Of writing –

It helps you conquer
Your thoughts.

It pins them to these pages
So they can't come after you.

When you've said
All you could
It frees you
            It frees your soul
            It frees your mind.

— Because even when love does not conquer all,
    Art will.

Each day is not a new day.
Each day is a product of yesterday.

Make sure yesterday was a good day,
And make today better.

— ~~Each day is a new day.~~

SERENA PATEL

There is something missing
In every room
I can't quite figure out what.

I check to make sure
Everything is still in place.

Maybe a book?
Maybe a vase?
What used to take up
This space?

Was it music?
Was it laughter?

— I can't seem to remember.

A masterpiece is not always pretty
Otherwise it would be called just that
But instead it is so much more.

It is all its imperfections
It is all its broken edges
It is every single one of its
Contradicting strokes.

Because it takes all of that
To make a masterpiece,

                    a masterpiece.

     — It is what it is.

There are flowers
Sprouting from her scars.

— Spring

IS THIS IT?

I write the way I loved
      With all of me and

                    deeply.

— About The Author

For more from Serena Patel:
www.facebook.com/serenapatelwriter
www.instagram.com/serena____patel